Though we travel the world over
carry it with us or we would find

A traveler without knowledge is a bird without wings.

—SA'DI

The world is a great book ... they who never stir
from home read only a page. —St. Augustine

My favorite thing is to go where I have never gone.

—DIANE ARBUS

A good traveler has no fixed plans and is not intent on arriving.

—LAO TZU

I like terra firma—the more firma, the less terra.

—GEORGE S. KAUFMAN

A pleasant companion reduces the length of the journey.

—PUBLILIUS SYRUS

I have wandered all
my life, and I have
also traveled;
the difference between
the two being this,
that we wander
for distraction,
but we travel
for fulfillment.

—HILAIRE BELLOC

Travel is fatal to prejudice, bigotry and narrow-mindedness.

—ANONYMOUS

The sea that calls all things unto her calls me, and I must embark.
—KAHLIL GIBRAN

I have been a wanderer among distant fields.
I have sailed down mighty rivers. —PERCY BYSSHE SHELLEY

If an ass goes traveling, he'll not come home a horse.
—Thomas Fuller

A journey of a thousand miles begins with a single step.

—Confucius

It is good to have an end to journey towards; but it is the journey that matters, in the end. —URSULA K. LE GUIN

A man travels the world in search of what he needs
and returns home to find it. —GEORGE MOORE

[B]less not only the road but the bumps on the road. They are all part of the higher journey. —JULIA CAMERON

The man who goes
alone can start today;
but he who travels
with another
must wait till
the other is ready,
and it may
be a long time
before they get off.

—HENRY DAVID THOREAU, *WALDEN*

When you come to a fork in the road, take it.

—YOGI BERRA

It's where we go, and what we do when we get there.
that tells us who we are. —JOYCE CAROL OATES

Travelers never think that *they* are the foreigners.
—MASON COOLEY

Traveling is not just seeing
the new; it is also
leaving behind.
Not just opening doors;
also closing them behind you,
never to return.
But the place you have
left forever is always
there for you to see
whenever you shut your eyes.

—JAN MYRDAL

A wise traveler never despises his own country.

—CARLO GOLDONI

Travel is the best way we have of rescuing the humanity of places and saving them from abstraction and ideology.

—PICO IYER

The whole object of travel is not to set foot on foreign land;
it is at last to set foot on one's own country as a foreign land.

—G. K. CHESTERTON

The worst thing about being a tourist is having other tourists recognize you as a tourist. —RUSSELL BAKER

The world is a country which nobody ever yet knew by description;
one must travel through it one's self to be acquainted with it.

—LORD CHESTERFIELD

The thing I do most is
look at maps.
I study them.
If I'm going to a place,
I get all the maps and
look at them.
There's a lot of
information on a map.

—PAUL THEROUX

He who never leaves his country is full of prejudices.

—CARLO GOLDONI

I have found that there ain't no surer way to find out whether you like people or hate them than to travel with them. —MARK TWAIN

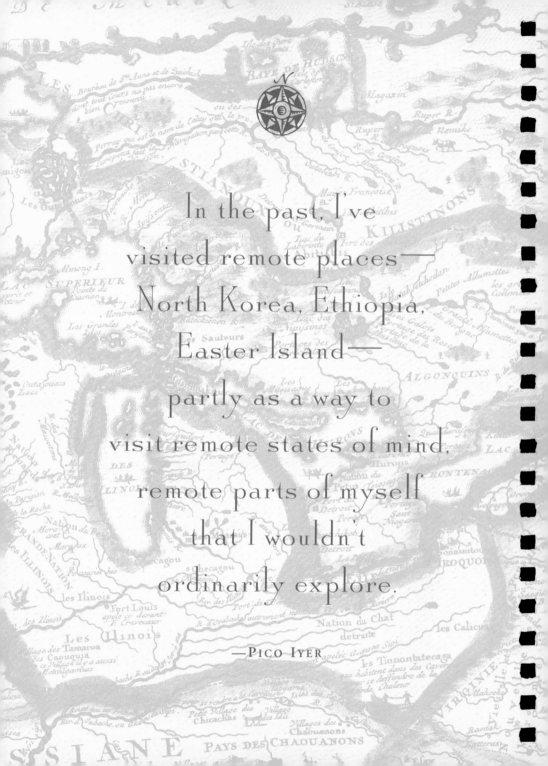

In the past, I've
visited remote places—
North Korea, Ethiopia,
Easter Island—
partly as a way to
visit remote states of mind,
remote parts of myself
that I wouldn't
ordinarily explore.

—PICO IYER

Travel is ninety per cent anticipation and ten per cent recollection.

—EDWARD STREETER

Wheresoever you go, go with all your heart.

—CONFUCIUS

I travel not to go anywhere, but to go. I travel for travel's sake. The great affair is to move. —ROBERT LOUIS STEVENSON

One sees great things from the valley; only small things from the peak. —G. K. CHESTERTON

There is only one journey. Going inside yourself.

—RAINER MARIA RILKE

Direct your eye right inward, and you'll find
A thousand regions in your mind
Yet undiscovered. Travel them, and be
Expert in home-cosmography.
—HENRY DAVID THOREAU

I find the great thing
in this world is not so
much where we stand,
as in what direction
we are moving:
To reach the port of
heaven, we must sail
sometimes with the wind
and sometimes against it,
but we must sail,
and not drift,
nor lie at anchor.

—OLIVER WENDELL HOLMES, JR.

Peculiar travel suggestions are dancing lessons from God.

—KURT VONNEGUT, JR.